D1413297

Essential Events

The Salem Witch Trials

Essential Events

The Salem Witch Trials

by Kekla Magoon

Content Consultant
Alison D'Amario
Director of Education
Salem Witch Museum

ABDO
Publishing Company

CREDITS

Published by ABDO Publishing Company, 8000 West 78th Street, Edina, Minnesota 55439.

Printed in the United States.

Editor: Jill Sherman
Copy Editor: Paula Lewis
Interior Design and Production: Emily Love
Cover Design: Emily Love

Library of Congress Cataloging-in-Publication Data
Magoon, Kekla.
The Salem witch trials / Kekla Magoon.
p. cm. — (Essential events)
Includes bibliographical references.
ISBN 978-1-60453-049-0
1. Trials (Witchcraft)—Massachusetts—Salem—History—17th century—Juvenile literature. 2. Witchcraft—Massachusetts—Salem—Juvenile literature. I. Title.

BF1576.M33 2008
133.4'3097445—dc22

2007031211

TABLE OF CONTENTS

Chapter 1

A woman testifies before the court in Massachusetts Bay Colony.

Turning Point

In the year 1692, in Salem Village, Massachusetts, strange and unexplainable events started to occur. Young girls began having disturbing "fits." They would fall on the floor, shaking and trembling in seizures, or sit and stare off into space, unaware of the world around them. They would cry and shout curses uncontrollably and scream if anyone touched them. The villagers grew terrified as more and more girls fell victim to these fits. Doctors could not explain it. No illness they knew of would cause such symptoms. But the fits continued and more girls became affected. The Puritan villagers began to believe that the girls had been possessed by the devil. They also feared someone in the community was practicing witchcraft.

The Afflicted Girls

Betty Parris and her cousin Abigail Williams were the first to fall ill in January 1692. Betty was just nine years old. Her father, the Reverend Samuel Parris, was the preacher at the village church. Eleven-year-old Abigail lived with the Parris family. The girls may have played around with fortune-telling and folk magic in the months before the fits began, so the idea of witchcraft was not new to them.

Betty's and Abigail's illnesses deeply upset people. Soon after, other girls began to have similar symptoms. The villagers wanted to

Salem Today

The area that was known as Salem Village in 1692 is now called Danvers, Massachusetts.

know what was causing these afflictions. Doctors could not determine the cause, but the villagers believed it must be the work of witches.

As the illness spread, Reverend Parris preached fiery sermons condemning the devil and anyone who worked on the devil's behalf. Puritans were a religious community and they believed the devil could influence people's behavior. They believed the devil could exercise control over the weak. Parris led the community in prayer vigils, and

Prayer Effort

Deodat Lawson was a minister who came into Salem Village to assist Reverend Parris with the prayer effort against the supposed witchcraft. Lawson recorded some of his observations from this stay in Salem:

> *[A]fter I came to my lodging, Captain [Jonathan] Walcott's daughter, Mary [age seventeen] came to Lt. Ingersoll's and spoke to me but suddenly after, as she stood by the door, was bitten so that she cried out of her wrist and looking on it with a candle, we saw apparently the marks of teeth both upper and lower set on each side of her wrist.*
>
> *In the beginning of the evening I went to give Mr. Parris a visit. When I was there his kinswoman, Abigail Williams (about 12 years of age), had a grievous fit. She was at first hurried with violence to and fro in the room (though Mrs. Ingersoll endeavored to hold her), sometimes making as if she would fly, stretching up her arms as high as she could and crying "Whish, whish, whish!" several times. ... After that, she run to the fire and begun to throw fire brands about the house and run against the back as if she would run up [the] chimney, and, as they said, she had attempted to go into the fire in other fits.*[1]

people fasted and worshipped in the hope that God would lift the curse off the girls. Nothing worked.

Several older girls, including Ann Putnam, Mercy Lewis, Elizabeth Hubbard, and Mary Walcott also started having fits. The villagers began to try to identify the witches who were causing the problem. These afflicted teenage girls were old enough to testify against the accused in court, which young Betty and Abigail alone could not. But none of the girls would tell who had cursed them.

Naming Witches

Two slaves lived in the Parris household: Tituba and Indian John. A villager named Mary Sibley slipped the slaves an old English recipe for a "witch cake." Using rye meal and urine from the sick girls, Tituba and Indian John baked the witch cake, then they fed it to a dog. Supposedly, the witches would be revealed.

The witch cake did not reveal any witches. If anything, the fits grew worse once the "spell" was complete. The girls writhed in pain, twisting

The Witch Cake

When Reverend Parris learned about the witch cake Tituba and Indian John baked, the reverend was furious. He scolded Mary Sibley for suggesting such an evil effort. Parris punished Tituba and Indian John for carrying out the plan. He believed that a spell to identify witchcraft was the same as practicing witchcraft.

and screaming. Sometimes they had to be held down to keep from hurting themselves. The villagers demanded that the girls tell them who was tormenting them.

Examination

Magistrates John Hathorne and Jonathan Corwin examined Sarah Good. After the examination, Hathorne commented, "Then desired the children, all of them, to look upon her, and see, if this were the person that had hurt them and so they all did look upon her and said this was one of the persons that did torment them—presently they were all tormented."[2]

Soon, the girls began naming names. They shouted some names during their fits and whispered others calmly afterward. Tituba, Sarah Good, and Sarah Osborne were the first named. Sarah Good was a beggar woman living in Salem, and Sarah Osborne was a feisty widow. Since both women were social outcasts, no one was surprised to think that they might be witches. The same was true for the slave, Tituba, whose West Indian ancestry made the villagers suspect her of practicing a form of voodoo, a Haitian religion. Determined to put a stop to the witchcraft, the villagers arrested the three accused women.

On March 1, 1692, court officers interviewed Sarah Good and Sarah Osborne. Both women denied the charges. They claimed not to have done anything to the girls. That same day, Tituba confessed that the devil had asked her to hurt the girls. She said she had resisted his advances, but she knew witchcraft did occur in the village. She hinted that several other people in the community were practicing witchcraft and conspiring against the children.

The villagers might have been satisfied with those first three arrests, if not for Tituba's testimony. Instead of ending the problem, her words stirred up more trouble. A witch hunt began in full force. The girls, and soon other villagers, named many people as witches. The terrified community desperately wanted the crisis to end. They set up a special court to put the accused on trial. According to the Bible, anyone found guilty of practicing witchcraft would be put to death: "Thou shalt not suffer a witch to live."[3]

A horrific series of events occurred over the next several

Voodoo

Historians have often remarked on the possibility that Tituba, being of West Indian ancestry, may have practiced some form of voodoo in the community. However, voodoo is a Haitian religion, and Tituba was from Barbados. It has also been speculated that she might have shared this practice with several of the girls in secret meetings in the Parrises' kitchen. Betty Parris, Abigail Williams, Mercy Lewis, and Mary Wolcott are some of the girls suspected of participating in these occult circles. However, there is no historical proof that these meetings ever occurred.

months. As many as 144 people were identified as witches and jailed. Of these, 19 were found guilty and hanged, and several others died in prison. When the hysteria calmed down, the people of Salem had to face the possibility that it had all been a mistake.

The Salem witch trials continue to fascinate people, even today, more than 300 years later. How and why did an event like this happen? And, what really caused the girls' fits so many years ago?

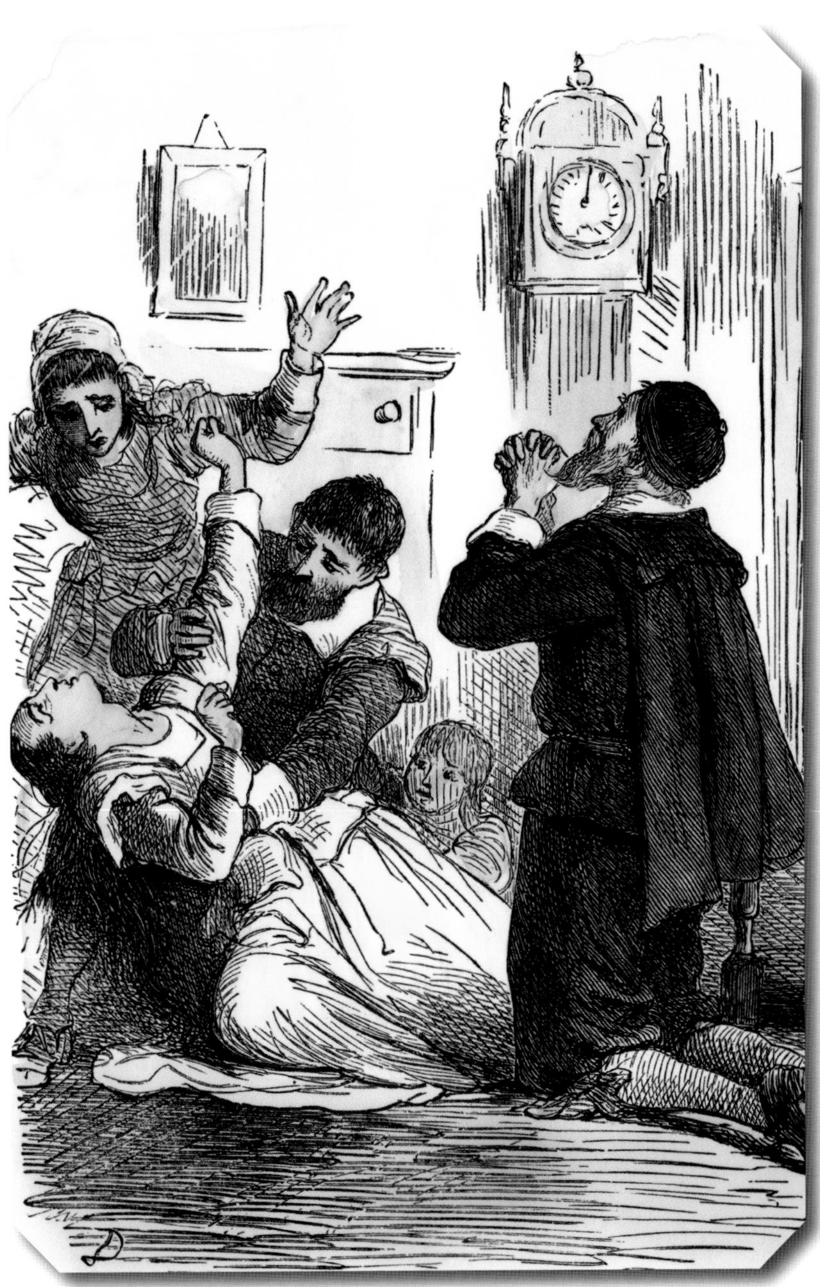

Young girls began to fall ill from a strange affliction in Salem, Massachusetts.

Chapter 2

Puritan leader Oliver Cromwell

Social Context

At the time of the Salem witch trials, Massachusetts was still a British colony. The events surrounding the Salem witch trials occurred almost 100 years before the colonies became a nation. Life for people in the colony of Massachusetts was very different from life today.

Salem

Salem was first settled in 1626 by Puritans who were seeking a safe place to practice their strict religious beliefs. Their beliefs about personal faith, worship, and church government set them apart. In England, some Puritans felt pressure to change their beliefs to match the more popular religions. Others unsuccessfully attempted to change the mainstream religions to follow Puritan beliefs. Throughout the 1600s, Puritan families traveled to the American colonies so they could practice their faith free from the judgment of others.

However, most Puritans remained loyal to the Church of England. Puritans retained many of the legal and social practices of

Salem Population

The official population of Salem Village in 1692 was 550 people in 90 households. Slaves, indentured servants, and the homeless were not counted, so the actual population was somewhat higher.

their homeland. These included British laws on witchcraft.

Puritan Faith

The term "Puritan" was first used in Great Britain in the late 1500s, following the Protestant Reformation. This was a time when religious leaders such as John Calvin and John Wyclif led a reform against the Roman Catholic Church. In particular, they believed the pope and priests had too much influence and power. In 1534, King Henry VIII denied the power of the pope because the Roman Catholic Church would not allow him to annul (or void) his marriage. With the Act of Supremacy, Henry VIII founded the Church of England, making himself the head of the church.

Puritans were English Christians who disagreed with some policies within the Church of England, even after the Reformation. They called themselves Puritans because they claimed that they wanted to purify the church. Puritans believed that church government should be based on the Bible and structured according to specific passages in the New Testament.

In the 1600s, Puritans strongly opposed the ruling powers of King James. A civil war, called the Puritan Revolution, broke out in the country. Led by Oliver Cromwell, the Puritans took control of the government in 1649. The Puritans lost power when Cromwell died in 1658.

Throughout the 1600s, approximately 10,000 Puritans left England to settle in the American colonies. This was called the Great Migration.

Salem Village was made up of a collection of neighboring farms, located near Salem Town. Salem Town was an important seaport town with a lot of business and trade. The nearby farms were originally considered part of Salem Town, but they broke off to form their own village. Still, the governments of the village and the town were closely linked. Farmers from the village sold their crops in the town.

In 1692, Salem Village had a population of approximately 600 people. Many local families worshipped at the Salem Village Church ministered by Samuel Parris. The largest building in town was the meetinghouse at the village center.

Changes in Society

The system of families living and working on independent farms was rapidly changing. People stopped bartering informally and began more formal purchasing practices. In the old system, one person might trade a jar of milk for a pouch of eggs. Families and communities grew their own crops to eat and drank the milk from their own animals. They sustained themselves without much outside help.

Under the new system, people would sell their milk for money, then use the money to buy eggs. Families and communities became part of a larger system that involved more trade and partnership with other cities and regions far from where they lived.

For farmers, this was a difficult transition. They were not used to dealing on a cash basis. By town standards they were mostly poor, even if their farms were successful. For many, entering the unfamiliar marketplaces of Salem Town was very stressful.

Salem, Massachusetts

Tension in Salem

Problems arose between people comfortable with the town and marketplace and people who wanted to keep the traditional farm life. Residents of Salem Village who lived close to Salem Town often were interested in town politics, business, and economics. The residents who lived farther from town were more interested in happenings within the village and at the frontier to the north and west. Tension grew between these two different sides of the community—tensions that affected everyday life in Salem Village.

These tensions also affected Salem Village politics. Salem Village leaders had to deal with the interests of the two factions, and it made governing the town more difficult. People who lived closer to the town were more aligned with town politics. Those deeper in the village wanted to distance themselves from the town. People remained loyal to their friends and to their neighbors. These divisions were probably somewhat similar to modern political parties, though they were not as formal. When witchcraft accusations began, these divisions often dictated who were the accusers and who were the accused.

Indian Wars

For the most part, people in Salem and other frontier settlers in New England coexisted peacefully with the Native American peoples living nearby. Occasionally, conflicts broke out between the British and various Native American tribes. In 1675, the Wabanaki people launched a surprise attack on a settlement in Maine as part of King Philip's War. In 1688, a second, shorter conflict broke out in the same area. Settlers in Maine were forced to flee, leaving behind their homes, property, and animals.

Hundreds of displaced settlers fled to Massachusetts.

Just as the Salem witch crisis was beginning, a band of Wabanaki people attacked the town of York, Maine. Many people died or were captured. Reinforcements came from New Hampshire to help the people of York, but they were too late. The damage had been done and another war with the Native Americans had begun.

Salem residents were aware of these conflicts, and it made them quite nervous. They lived in a heightened state of alert. The constant fear may have helped the witchcraft crisis spin out of control.

War in Maine

As the third Indian War broke out in Maine in 1692, George Burroughs wrote to leaders in the Massachusetts Bay Colony to let them know of the sorrowful events that had occurred in the North. He wrote, "God is still manifesting his displeasure against this Land, he who formerly hath set his hand to help us, doth even write bitter things against us."[1]

Burroughs did not yet know that young girls in Salem were strangely afflicted and that the villagers had begun to fear evil spirits were at work. His words could only have worried them about their own situation.

The Church in Salem Village

In 1672, James Bayley moved from Boston to serve as the first minister in Salem Village. He stayed in the community for eight years, which was not a lengthy time

Residents of Salem Town were interested in the politics of Boston, Massachusetts, a busy port.

for a minister. The villagers had been divided on their opinions of how Bayley managed the church.

Salem Village had three more ministers before the witchcraft crisis. George Burroughs came from Maine and was minister for three years before returning north to his home. Deodat Lawson followed as the minister for four years, before he moved on to Boston. In 1689, three years before the witch trials, Salem Village welcomed a new minister, Samuel Parris.

Return to Salem

Deodat Lawson returned to Salem during the witchcraft crisis to try to help. George Burroughs also returned to Salem, but many of the villagers did not like him and quickly accused him of being a witch.

Samuel Parris's Ministry

Samuel Parris and his family came to Salem from Boston. Originally from England, Parris had also lived in Barbados, an island in the West Indies. Parris would serve at the Salem Village Church. The village now had a formal church with an ordained minister. Many of the villagers were pleased with the change and wanted to show Salem Town that they were becoming an independent village.

However, some villagers were unhappy with this decision. Those who remained interested in Salem Town did not want to remove themselves from it. Samuel Parris's actions in Salem only added to the problems. As he set up the Salem Village Church, he made it clear that church membership was very important. Still, only about one-fourth of the Salem residents joined. Church members were mostly from farms far from Salem Town, the people who wanted Salem to be a totally separate village.

Parris enforced special rules that gave church members privileges in the community, and he treated worship as an exclusive event. Nonmembers could attend the church services and hear his sermons, but he made them leave the meetinghouse before he served communion, and he refused to baptize their children. Many people in Salem did not like him. They began to organize plans to force him to leave town.

One Sunday in January 1692, Parris gave a particularly fiery

Biblical Passages

The Puritans heeded Biblical passages that spoke of witchcraft and evil. Reverend Parris made sure his congregation was aware of passages such as these:

"Be sober, be vigilant; because your adversary the devil, as a roaring lion, walketh about, seeking whom he may devour."[2]

—I Peter 5:8

"Thou shalt not suffer a witch to live."[3]

—Exodus 22:18

sermon about the devil's ability to work in and through people. He suggested that the people who refused to join the church were letting themselves be instruments for evil in the world. Just a few days later, Parris's daughter Betty and his niece Abigail began showing strange symptoms.

Church in Salem

Chapter 3

Salem residents believed that women were practicing witchcraft.

Historical Persecution of Witches

Throughout history, the idea of a witch has been perceived in many different ways. In various cultures and belief systems, witches have been revered, feared, persecuted, or met with disdain and disbelief. Their perceived skills in magic, potions, spells, and curses have been received as blessings, objects of curiosity, or hated abilities. Nearly every culture includes music and religion as well as some elements of supposed witchcraft.

Origins of Witchcraft

Belief in witches and the practice of witchcraft stretches back to ancient times. Witchcraft evolved from the earliest societies, whose pagan beliefs centered on fertility and the mysteries of the earth. Ancient Egyptians believed in supernatural power. Greek and Roman mythology are full of magical creatures and events. The faith systems of African, Asian, and Native American societies included witchcraft long before the establishment of many of the major religions we know today.

Ancient cultures all over the world believed that some people had the ability to cast spells, create potions, and bring help or harm to others using supernatural powers. Not all

The Evil Eye

Belief in witchcraft has led to a wide variety of superstitions that still exist. Many cultures in Europe and the Near East fear the power of "the evil eye." This power enables witches to curse and bring harm to people just by looking at them. In Western culture, the phrase "giving someone the evil eye" has retained its ancient meaning of wishing someone harm.

societies called these people witches. Names such as sorcerer, conjurer, witch doctor, and healer were often used.

Historians know that people have believed in witches for a long time because much has been written about them over time. Many fairy tales have a witch as a main character. Several Shakespeare plays include witches and magical creatures as characters. Classic works of literature such as *The Odyssey* and *Beowulf* also feature witches. Folk stories from all areas of the Middle East, Africa, Europe, Asia, and North and South America tell of sorcerers, witches, and magical occurrences. Even the Bible makes references to witches and witchcraft.

Good Witches

Witches were not always considered to be evil. Most cultures that believed in witches believed in both good and bad witches. In many ancient cultures, those who were viewed as witches lived within the community. People approached a good witch for help with a problem. In turn, the witch would cast a spell to heal or to bring good fortune. A mother with a sick baby might seek a potion to heal the child. A farmer would ask for a cow that had stopped giving milk to be cured. A young wife would seek advice or treatment for an easy childbirth.

These witches were usually women with ancient knowledge of healing, likely with herbal treatments. They were feared because of their power but also respected for their abilities. They made teas, creams, lotions, and potions that helped relieve many simple ailments. The treatments seemed mysterious but often worked.

Today, witches' healing powers might not be so impressive.

Jeanne d'Arc

In 1424, a young French woman named Jeanne d'Arc (Joan of Arc) began hearing voices and seeing visions. The 13-year-old Jeanne believed the voices were those of Saint Michael, Saint Catherine, and Saint Margaret speaking to her from heaven. She listened to the voices for five years before they told her of her mission.

The voices told her to protect the prince, the Dauphin Charles, from English invaders as he went to the city of Reims for his coronation ceremony. Jeanne followed the voices. She convinced a council of church leaders that the prince needed her help.

On April 29, 1429, still following the voices, Jeanne led the army into battle along the Loire River valley until the path to Reims was clear. The Dauphin Charles was able to enter Reims and be crowned king.

Jeanne fought for the king for over a year. In May 1430, she was captured in the town of Compeigne. She was turned over to the English in November. Jeanne was condemned as a witch and heretic because she had worked with King Charles, whose authority the English did not recognize.

Jeanne d'Arc was burned at the stake in Rouen, France, on May 30, 1431. In 1456, a separate court overturned the ruling from her trial. In 1920, the Roman Catholic Church declared her a saint.

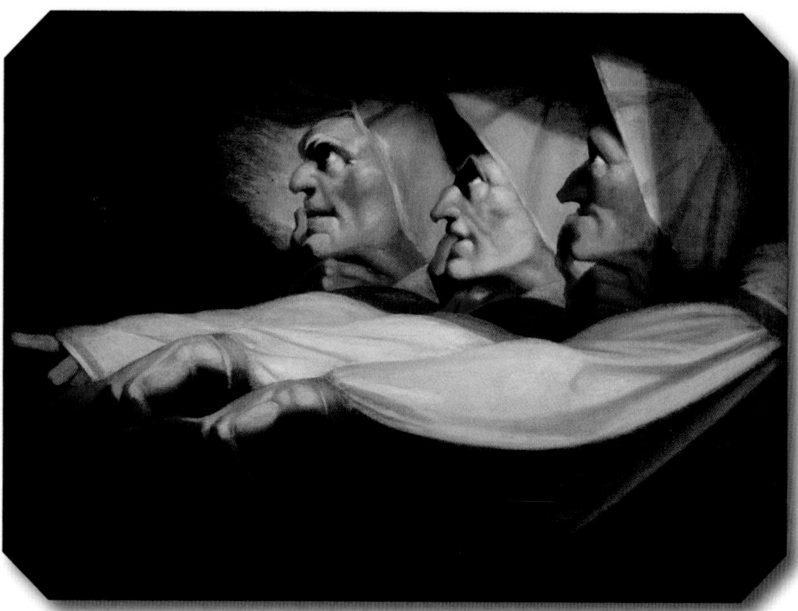

Often, witches were believed to be old, ugly, and unkempt.

Herbal treatments such as putting aloe on a burn or eating mint to help with digestion have proven medical benefits. However, certain other witchcraft treatments are unlikely to have been more than a placebo—working because of the person's belief that it would work.

Witch Symbolism

In the United States today, fewer people believe in witchcraft. Still, the common image of a witch remains as that of an old person with yellow or greenish skin, a long warty nose, wild hair, a pointy black hat, black robes and a broom, a cauldron, and a black cat. Even very small children can recognize a witch by these characteristics.

These familiar images are the result of a long history of believing in witches. In the times when witch hunts were common, the accused people tended to look something like the stereotype. They were usually older women who were community outcasts and often poor and unkempt. Drawings of witches portrayed them as ugly and warty to show that they were unpleasant and undesirable. Warts were also believed to be marks of the devil upon witches.

Pictures of witches often have red or orange backgrounds, which represent the fires of hell. Witches are shown dressed in black, a color that is used to symbolize evil, as

Halloween

Halloween is celebrated each year on October 31, the night before All Saints Day on November 1. Halloween has its origins in the ancient Celtic fire festival called "Samhain." It marks the change from summer to winter. Celts believed that the worlds of the living and the dead were closest on Samhain.

Halloween was originally called All Hallows' Eve. On that night, it was believed that evil spirits were released from hell to walk the earth. People dressed up in scary costumes to frighten the spirits back into their world. This ensured that when the saints arrived the following day, there would be no evil spirits to interfere.

Witchcraft Act of 1604

The Witchcraft Act of 1604 that was passed in England made the practice of witchcraft illegal and punishable by death without the benefit of a clergyman. The law detailed some acts of witchcraft that would be considered felonies, such as communing with spirits. The act affected all of England and its colonies, including those in the Americas. The act was repealed in 1735. Fortune-telling and communing with the dead were still illegal but punishable only with fines and jail time. This act was not repealed until 1951.

well as nighttime, when witches supposedly do their work. Black cats are often associated with witches and were believed to be their helpers. Cauldrons represent the mysterious potions and spells that witches brew.

Pointy objects such as brooms can be symbols of men and masculinity. Witches were often accused of trying to act like men. According to legends, brooms were also a way for witches to travel. This concept frightened people because the idea of flight was foreign and magical. They feared that witches flew off in the night to meet and plot against good citizens. It was unusual for women to speak their opinions loudly in public or run their own households. Those accused of witchcraft were often independent women who spoke their minds.

Witchcraft in Europe and New England

In the 1600s, several witch hunts occurred in Europe. People in countries such as France, Spain,

Italy, and England accused others of witchcraft. Thousands of people, mostly women, died in witch hunts across the continent. In these cases, gossip and rumors were generally allowed as proof of witchcraft. Any person who was feared or disliked could be accused of witchcraft and killed without any proof or evidence of what he or she had done. By the early 1700s, witch hunts in Europe had lost popularity and were less common.

Prior to the Salem incidents, there had been numerous other witch hunts in New England. The earliest witchcraft executions in the colonies occurred in the 1640s. The Puritan belief in witches along with the prevalence of diseases and accidents that they did not understand led the Puritans to blame strange occurrences on witchcraft. People had been accused of witchcraft—and some were executed—in Massachusetts, Connecticut, and the surrounding colonies.

In many cases, a witch hunt was brought on by events such as a child falling to an unexplained illness or a season of bad crops. Unable to explain the events, the townspeople would suspect witchcraft. After one or two people had been accused and found guilty of witchcraft, the public would calm down, believing they had eradicated the problem. People believed the guilty had been punished, so the witch hunt would end—for a time.

The Salem witch hunt became notable because it did not stop with one or two accusations. So many girls were affected by the strange illness and so many people were accused that the crisis grew.

End of Executions

The last witchcraft execution in England occurred in 1716. Mary and Elizabeth Hicks, mother and daughter, were hanged. Throughout the rest of Europe, the practice of executing witches ended by the mid-eighteenth century.

People feared the possible existence of witches.

Chapter 4

People believed Tituba told witchcraft tales to children.

Afflictions Emerge

The Salem witch crisis developed after several girls became very sick with a strange illness. The community accepted witchcraft as a fact of life. That belief led them to assume the affliction was brought on by witches. The girls' alarming illness may have inspired the witch hunt, but it was the adults around them who conducted the hunt.

Playing with the Occult

A group of girls in Salem experimented with fortune-telling and little occult spells that they had heard of. They hid their actions from their parents and other adults because it would have been frowned upon. Puritan adults were afraid of the occult, witchcraft, and magic. Anything similar to it was forbidden. Perhaps that made it exciting for the girls, as they had very few other outlets for silliness and play in their strict community.

The girls' fortune-telling experiments were simple enough. They played with spells to determine what their future lives would be like, who they would marry, or how they would fall in love. They may have stumbled onto something in folk magic that scared them or read an omen in their fortune-telling games that they thought meant something bad.

Strange Symptoms

Abigail Williams and little Betty Parris began having strange fits in January 1692. Betty would sit for hours staring vacantly into space and would be

In Puritan jails, people were allowed to read the Bible.

startled if anyone spoke to her. Abigail began falling on the floor in seizures.

Reverend Parris called a doctor in to help the girls. Dr. William Griggs came to observe Betty and Abigail. He could not determine what was causing their ailments. He told Reverend Parris that it might be a witch's curse.

Reverend Parris enlisted the support of the church to pray for the girls to get well. The illness only became worse. The girls continued having fits for more than a month. Soon, other girls in the town began falling into similar fits. It was a strange occurrence that frightened many people. Eight village girls were afflicted: Abigail Williams, Betty Parris, Ann Putnam, Mercy Lewis, Elizabeth Hubbard, Mary Wolcott, Mary Warren, and Betty Pope. The girls' symptoms included lethargy, seizures, temporary paralysis, and distraction. Their skin showed bite marks and pinches; they also felt pinpricks. The girls were observed cursing uncontrollably, barking, and with their eyes rolling back and to the sides. At times, their arms and legs twisted. They also spoke of hallucinations or "spectral visions." Puritans believed that the devil could use a witch's shape to harm others and to seduce followers.

It was not just the girls and young women of Salem who were affected by the strange illness. Adult men also experienced symptoms. Perhaps to preserve their dignity, afflicted men were not made the center of attention. They related their experiences and even testified. Some were examined, but they did not generally receive the same attention that the women did.

Cattle and livestock on the farms in Salem also seemed to be ill. People reported strange incidents where cows would race around the fields as if mad or fall to the ground with twitching legs. Some animals died from the illness.

Eyewitnesses

A number of eyewitness accounts were recorded of the girls' symptoms and fits. The Salem crisis attracted a good deal of attention and many observers made records of the trials and the witch hunt as a whole. Numerous unofficial accounts of the crisis have emerged.

Deodat Lawson, Salem's former minister, returned to Salem Village during the witchcraft crisis. He stayed with Thomas Putnam's family, where he witnessed the fits of young Ann Putnam. He made detailed notes about what he had seen, and the symptoms alarmed him greatly. He stayed in Salem during the trials as somewhat of an impartial observer, though his views appear to have been in line with the court's.

John Hale, a minister in nearby Beverly, Massachusetts, also witnessed the events. He wrote his account, *A Modest Inquiry*, nearly ten years later, when he had the benefit of hindsight to tell the story. During the time of the trials, he was in favor of the proceedings and served as a witness in one of the cases. His later writings reflect sorrow over the events.

Suggestion of Witchcraft

It is not clear whether the girls initially believed that they were victims of witchcraft. The girls may have embraced the idea only after others in the village suggested that they were possessed by witches. It appears that it was not until after the idea was suggested that the girls began to speak of being tormented by women of the village. Reverend Parris and other clergy began asking the girls to identify the witches. At first the girls said nothing. Later, the girls named three women from the village as their tormentors: Sarah Good, Sarah Osborne, and Tituba.

Word began to spread that witchcraft might be to blame for the girls' odd behavior. The community was no longer willing to wait for prayers to heal the girls. They wanted to take action. On February 29, 1692, four men—Thomas Putnam, Edward Putnam, Joseph Hutchinson, and Thomas Preston—filed complaints with the local magistrates, John Hathorne and Jonathan Corwin. Hathorne and Corwin brought the accused women in for questioning.

Spectral Evidence

In most witchcraft cases, there was no hard evidence that an accused person had done anything wrong. Most testimony and eyewitness accounts were of the strange, unexplained behavior of the girls—not the actions of the accused. It is very difficult to prove that someone has practiced witchcraft by modern courtroom standards. Courtroom procedures at the time of the Salem witch trials were very different.

Spectral evidence was enough proof to cast suspicion on a possible witch. Spectral evidence meant that the victims could say they saw the likeness of the accused person hurting them or that they heard the voice of the accused. Although there was no proof of these occurrences, the Salem court decided to accept such claims as proof of witchcraft.

The girls also claimed that the witches used familiars to torment them. Familiars were animal attendants who helped witches do their work, often taking the form of small animals such as cats, birds, and squirrels. Familiars were also accepted as proof of witchcraft, which meant that a person who had seen the animal that was associated with a particular witch could accuse that person.

Examining Sarah Good and Sarah Osborne

Based on the word of the afflicted girls, Salem Village leaders brought Sarah Good and Sarah Osborne in to be questioned on March 1. The accused women were brought to the meetinghouse, which was the largest building in town. A crowd of

Sarah Good's Examination

One of the official scribes present at Sarah Good's examination wrote comments about her manner in his notes: "Her answers were in a very wicked, [spiteful] manner reflecting and retorting against the authority with base and abusive words and many lies."[1]

onlookers pressed into the room, eager to watch the proceedings. Two scribes recorded the events and wrote down the women's testimonies.

The girls were also brought in to identify their tormentors. Betty Parris and Abigail Williams were too young to serve as witnesses in the trial, but they were present. The testimony of the older girls, such as Ann Putnam and Elizabeth Hubbard, would count most.

John Hathorne, a local magistrate, conducted the interviews. He questioned Sarah Good and Sarah Osborne for hours. He asked questions such as, "How long have you been in the snare of the devil?" and "How did you hurt these girls?" and "What evil spirit have you familiarity with?"[2]

Sarah Good was interviewed first. She denied all charges of witchcraft for herself, but said that Sarah Osborne had probably done it. Later, Sarah Osborne tried to defend herself by suggesting that even though she was innocent, the devil could have

A Spouse's Betrayal

Sarah Good's husband, William, added to the suspicion by speaking out against her. He mentioned a new wart that had recently appeared on her body. He told the court that he suspected it might be the devil's mark on her.

used her likeness to torment the girls without her knowledge. Later, others accused of witchcraft would use this defense as well.

Tituba's Testimony

Tituba, the Parrises' slave, was also called in to be questioned. Unlike Sarah Good and Sarah Osborne, Tituba did not deny the witchcraft charges. She told the examiners that the devil had spoken to her, but she had ignored him. She told them that he had asked her to hurt the girls, but she refused. She also said that she knew of other witches. She told John Hathorne four women were involved. She told him they were, "Goody Osborne and Sarah Good and I do not know who the other were. Sarah Good and Osborne would have me hurt the children but I would not."[3]

Tituba's testimony frightened the Salem villagers. If not for her ominous words, the villagers might have ended the witch hunt with the three accused women. But by saying she knew of several witches meeting in secret, she drew the court's attention away from herself and put it out in the community. The witch hunt was on.

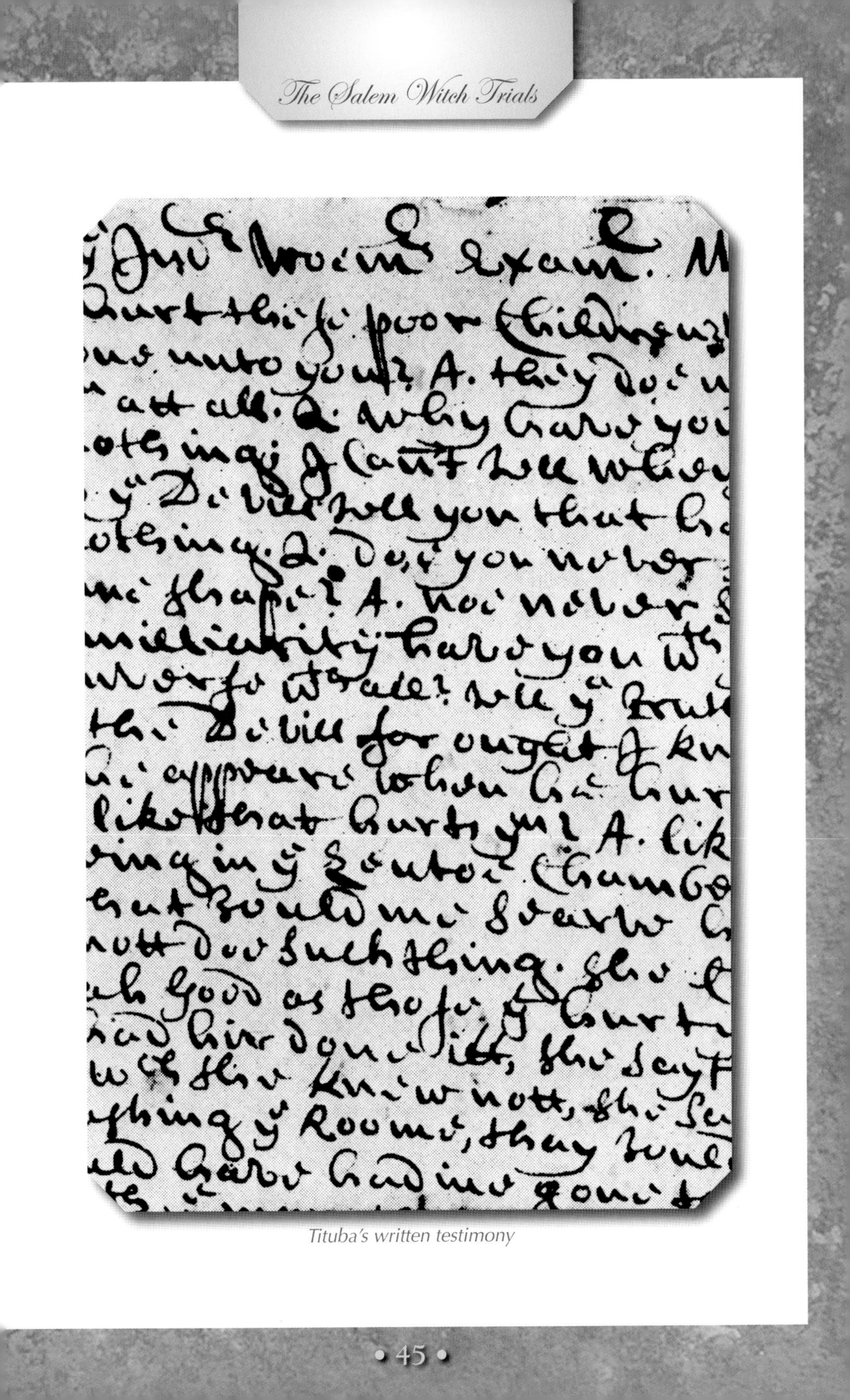

Tituba's written testimony

Chapter 5

A witness testifies at a witchcraft trial in Salem.

Naming Witches

Tituba's testimony deeply frightened the Salem villagers. They wanted to find these other witches and keep them from tormenting the girls, but they did not know who these other witches were. Tituba had named two women as witches, Sarah Good and Sarah Osborne, but suggested that several more existed. Many people fell under suspicion.

Questioned Again

The three accused women were put in jail after the first examination. During the next few days, the magistrates interviewed Sarah Good once, Sarah Osborne twice, and Tituba three times. These interviews were most likely conducted in private, perhaps right in the jail. The magistrates hoped to obtain more information and confessions from the women.

Sarah Good and Sarah Osborne did not change their testimony at all. Tituba, however, at the persistent questioning of the magistrates, gave more details about her talks with the devil. Tituba told John Hathorne that the devil had shown her a black book, where he kept lists of all the people in his service. She said that there were names in the book of people from Salem Village, Salem Town, and Boston. Tituba not only claimed that she put her mark in the black book but she also claimed to have seen Sarah Good and Sarah Osborne's marks.

Tituba also testified that she had seen familiars that belonged to witches. These small animal creatures were believed to help witches do their work. She spoke of seeing a winged-woman creature, a short hairy beast, a large black dog, a hog, several cats, and a yellow bird that she associated with Sarah Osborne. She told Hathorne that she had seen Sarah Osborne feeding the little bird out of her hand. Although Tituba continued to elaborate on the witchcraft she claimed to have seen, she did not offer any names other than Sarah Good's and Sara Osborne's.

In today's court system, Tituba's testimony would seem far-fetched. She offered no proof of the claims that she made and no one demanded any from her. The Salem community desperately wanted an explanation for the girls' strange afflictions and witchcraft was a good enough reason for them to believe Tituba.

Who Were the Accused?

The women who were accused of witchcraft tended to be older women, usually single or widowed, who were poor and perhaps even beggars. This was true not only in Salem but throughout New England. Sarah Good and Sarah Osborne were two such women. Sarah Good was indeed a beggar. Sarah

Osborne had been widowed some years back. She was now living, unmarried, with a man in her house. This was extremely scandalous behavior in a Puritan community. Few in Salem were surprised that these two women were accused. Some suspicion had existed in the village about these women's leanings toward the devil.

A typical New England witch hunt would have ended after Sarah Good and Sarah Osborne were identified, tried, and either jailed or executed. But after Tituba's confessions, the young girls were pressed to name

Singled Out

Those accused of witchcraft were generally poor outcasts in the community. There were, however, other types of women who were singled out during the witch hunts: those in authority. Women in authority were threatening to men in seventeenth-century New England. Quaker women preachers were the only female ministers of the day. They were often persecuted as witches because they dared to interpret the word of God. The more that an accused woman spoke out, even in her own defense, the harder it became to convince people of her innocence.

It was unusual for well-respected members of the community to be accused of witchcraft. Despite the general impression that Martha Corey and Rebecca Nurse were well respected in Salem Village, there may have been reasons for the accusations against them. Before she was married, Martha Corey had given birth to a mixed-race child. Even though she later became a member of the church, village gossips still spoke of her scandalous past.

Rebecca Nurse's accuser was Ann Putnam. Nurse's family had a history of problems with the Putnams. Historians suspect the family tension may have influenced Ann to name Rebecca Nurse as a witch.

other witches. The girls' fits continued, and they named two others from Salem Village: Elizabeth Proctor and Dorcas Good, the four-year-old daughter of Sarah Good. They, too, matched the typical profile of accused witches.

The Salem witch hunt quickly broke from the pattern of accusing outcasts. The afflicted girls began accusing women of good standing in the community. The next two women the girls named, Rebecca Nurse and Martha Corey, were well-respected, churchgoing women in Salem. In addition, a good number of the accused women had achieved some financial independence. Many had inherited property or stood to inherit property in the near future.

The Salem witch hunt took an unusual turn. The heightened level of fear in the village meant the villagers were willing to believe the girls' extreme accusations. During March and April, many more women were jailed as witches. The accusations had spread beyond the boundaries of Salem Village into the neighboring towns. By June, approximately 70 people had been accused. Salem leaders needed to find a way to deal with the problem.

The examinations of Sarah Good, Sarah Osborne, and Tituba were a standard response to witchcraft suspicions. The magistrates, Hathorne and Corwin, studied the information gained from the interviews to determine if there was enough evidence to put the women on trial.

> "Such was the darkness of that day, the tortures and lamentations of the afflicted, and the power of former precedents, that we walked in the clouds and could not see our way."[1]
>
> —*Reverend John Hale,* A Modest Inquiry

Powerful Women

Women who were financially independent or property owners had potential to be influential in the community. This was an unexpected and unusual position for a Puritan woman. Puritans may have felt threatened by or jealous of these powerful women. In Salem, these women were more commonly accused of witchcraft than other villagers.

Puritans believed that speech was a powerful force. Their culture valued preaching and education, both actions that involve speaking and knowledge. Puritans also placed men in positions of authority above women. Men were the preachers, teachers, and speakers that the Puritans wanted to hear. Women were expected to be quiet, respectful, and obedient to the men around them.

Women who spoke out of turn or with a haughty tone were considered "contrary." Female witches were accused of mumbling curses and faced extra suspicion if something bad occurred after they had been seen "muttering." Sarah Good was often accused of walking away from houses muttering curses, after her begging at the door had not resulted in food or help. Later, if a farm animal died or a child caught a cold, Sarah Good was blamed for causing the problem with her words.

Women who quarreled with others or raised their voices in public were considered threatening, particularly if they dared to challenge powerful men in the village. When the witch trials began, the judges often scolded the accused women for not being respectful to the men in court. The accused women were angry at the false accusations and grew frustrated that no one believed them. But a woman speaking strongly, even in her own defense, only raised suspicion in the court.

Witch Defenders

Not everyone in Salem supported the witch hunt. Many people believed that those considered to be witches were wrongly accused. It took a lot of courage to speak out against the witch hunt. People who supported the accused were often believed to be witches themselves, so very few people defended those who were accused.

A segment of the Salem population did stand up for the accused witches. John Proctor, a Salem Village farmer, spoke out against the trial proceedings. His wife, Elizabeth, was one of the first women to be accused. John Proctor wrote letters to ministers in Boston to tell them of the hysteria that was taking place in Salem. He pleaded with them to do something to help the accused women.

His support for the accused caused people such as Reverend Parris and the Putnam family to accuse Proctor of witchcraft. They reasoned that anyone who wanted the accused released must be one of them. John Proctor was arrested and jailed with his wife to await trial.

Literacy in Salem

Making one's mark in a book was the same as signing one's name. Most likely, many people in Salem Village were unable to read or write their own names. It was not necessary for farmers to read in order to do their work, so many of them did not learn. On important documents, instead of writing their name, people could simply put a mark, such as an "X," a check mark, or a squiggle to show that they agreed with what had been written.

Courts of Oyer and Terminer

The governor established the Court of Oyer and Terminer for Salem Village. The terms *Oyer* and *Terminer* are Anglo-French and mean "to hear and to determine."

When it became clear that there were more witches involved, the situation changed. The village leaders set out to find a better way to handle witchcraft accusations.

Hathorne and Corwin appealed to the new governor of the Massachusetts Bay Colony to set up a court. Sir William Phips had recently arrived from England to govern the colony. When Governor Phips heard about the many witches sitting in jail in Salem, he authorized a special trial process. The Court of Oyer and Terminer was established on May 27, 1692, to manage the witchcraft trials. Nine judges were assigned to the court. The court was scheduled to begin its session to try the first group of witches on June 2.

Many good Puritan women were accused of witchcraft in Salem.

Chapter 6

Reverend Stephen Burroughs is executed for witchcraft.

Hangings

On May 30, 1692, Judge Samuel Sewall put out a call for jury members. He sent notices to as many as 40 men. Sewall was able to secure 12 men to hear the cases. The jury members were to sit and listen to the evidence presented in court, then make their determination. The Court of Oyer and Terminer would convene on June 2.

Debating Spectral Evidence

Nine judges were selected to preside over the witchcraft trials. Before the trials could begin, the judges needed to make a decision concerning the use of spectral evidence. Some of the judges thought that such rumors should not be allowed as proof of witchcraft. They believed that the devil could be using the accused people's likenesses without their knowledge. Others thought it was good evidence. They believed the accused had to be instruments of the devil for their specters, or spirits, to be used. During these debates, no one questioned the truth of the girls' visions but only what the visions actually could prove.

The judges studied previous witchcraft cases and legal writings to help them make their decision. It was an important decision, because spectral evidence would be the main source of proof in most of the cases. Without the girls' visions as evidence, the judges knew it would be difficult or even impossible to prove who was responsible for the supposed witchcraft. They believed that witchcraft was occurring, but they wanted to be sure they had absolutely proven each person's guilt before pronouncing a death sentence.

The court decided to accept spectral testimony, but it preferred for the girls' stories to be backed up by witnesses. This meant that if people had seen the afflicted girl in the middle of a fit, the visions the girl claimed to see could be used in court, even if the witnesses had not seen the vision. Scholars today find this legal decision disturbing because the careful decision-making process that the judges went through still brought them to a strange conclusion. Their decision led to many unfair deaths and was later recognized as a mistake.

Moles and birthmarks counted as proof of the devil's mark on the suspected witches' bodies. Before each trial, a special jury examined the accused for markings. A female jury looked at the bodies of accused women. A male jury looked at the accused men. The jury members would then testify to the court about any marks they found.

The Trials Begin

During each trial, at least five of the judges had to be present to hear the case. The court officials were men with a lot of legal experience. Thomas Newton was appointed attorney general and served as the prosecutor. He was also an experienced lawyer. The accused would be allowed to speak in their own defense. Defense lawyers were not used at this time.

Judges at Salem

For the most part, the judges for the Court of Oyer and Terminer were men who already believed in the witchcraft epidemic. Nathanial Saltonstall was the only reluctant participant, and he resigned from the court shortly after Bridget Bishop was sentenced to death. He was uncomfortable with some actions of the court.

Because the evidence against Bridget Bishop was very strong, the magistrates decided to hear her case first, on June 2. All the evidence presented against Bridget Bishop was from five or six years prior to when the girls became afflicted. She had long been suspected of witchcraft in the village, but the magistrates had never believed there was enough evidence to try her case. That changed during the witch trial crisis. The old fears grew stronger and the community felt an urgent need to get rid of anyone connected to witchcraft. The court sentenced Bridget Bishop to death.

Court Proceedings

In the courtroom, 11 people testified including several of the afflicted girls. They told about their fits and the spectral visions they had seen. Often, they fell into fits in the courtroom. They did not have to testify about those fits. It was assumed the witches in the room were torturing the girls to keep them from speaking.

Next, other witnesses testified about what they had seen. The girls' parents and neighbors described the fits and hysteria. Farmers who had lost cattle to a strange illness claimed the accused were responsible. Village residents told about odd things that happened to them when the accused witches were around. Several husbands testified against their wives in order to avoid suspicion. Accused witches who testified against their fellow prisoners may have done so to protect themselves.

Salem villagers believed that witches were unable to recite Bible passages or speak prayers aloud. They often asked the accused to recite their favorite Bible verse during the trial. If they could not, or if they stumbled over a word, it was believed to be the work of the devil within them.

Finally, the accused witches were allowed to speak in their own defense. Many firmly denied the accusations of witchcraft but were unable to convince the court. Some of the accused broke down and confessed to being in the devil's snare. Puritans considered any sin to be a pact with the devil. Under the court's questioning of their previous sins, many of the accused may have understood even their minor sins as proof of wrongdoing and confessed. Witchcraft was a capital crime in the colony. If found guilty, the accused could be executed. They may have confessed so that the court would be lenient in the sentencing. The magistrates put the confessors in jail, hoping that they would name other witches. This reaction was unique to the Salem crisis. In the past, a confession was often a death sentence. Once it became clear that the confessors were not being executed, more of the accused began to confess as well. Only those who denied the charges of witchcraft were executed.

"Not Guilty"

Several times during the trials, the jury returned "not guilty" verdicts. They were immediately asked by the judges to reconsider the decision.

The Hangings

The Court of Oyer and Terminer met five times during the summer and fall of 1692. On June 10, 1692, Bridget Bishop became the first accused witch to be hanged on Gallows Hill. A large crowd of people came to witness the hanging.

On June 28 and June 29, the court met for a second time and tried Rebecca Nurse, Sarah Good, and three other women. All were sentenced to death. All five maintained their innocence all the way to the gallows. Each was allowed to make a final speech, but none confessed the sin of witchcraft.

At the gallows, four of the five accused women prayed for God to forgive the villagers, but Sarah Good did not. A local minister, Reverend Nicholas Noyes, said that her lack of prayers only confirmed that she was a witch. Sarah Good replied, "I am no more a witch than you are a wizard, and if you take away my life, God will give you blood to drink."[1]

Some onlookers in the crowd began to doubt the women's guilt because they failed to repent before they were hanged. Puritan beliefs should have led guilty people to beg for forgiveness in their last moments if they wanted any chance to go to heaven. Many of the villagers worried about this, but most did not dare speak up. The five women were executed together on July 19.

The third trial occurred from August 2 to August 6. Salem Village's former minister, George Burroughs, was sentenced to death, along with John Proctor, Elizabeth Proctor, and three others. Five till this 31 May 1692 at the same moment that I was hear[ing] evidence read by the honoured Magistrats to take my Oath I was ag[ain] re-assaulted & tortured by my before mentioned Tormentor Rebekah [illegible]

Sworne Salem Village May the 3[illegible] 1692 Before us John Hathorne Jonathan Corwin

[illegible] Putnam senior [illegible] before us the Justices of [illegible] and owned this her evidence 3 d of June 1692

The testimony of Ann Putnam junr witnesseth & saith that being [illegible] when her mother was afflicted she saw Martha Kory Sarah [illegible] & Rebekah Nurse or their apparition upon her mother

Testified to ye truth thereof by Ann Putnam Salem May. 31st. 1692 Before us John Hathorne Jonathan Corwin

Reproduction of Ann Putnam's deposition

of the condemned witches were hanged. Elizabeth Proctor was spared from death because she was pregnant, and the court did not want to punish the innocent child along with its mother. George Burroughs attempted to save his life by reciting the Lord's Prayer as he stood in the gallows, about to be hanged. He spoke each word of the prayer perfectly, so some people believed he should be released. However, one of the officials made a stirring speech to the crowd to convince them that it was a trick of witchcraft and the hanging proceeded.

The fourth trial was held on September 9. Six accused women, including Martha Corey and Mary Easty, and two men were sentenced to death. Mary Easty wrote a letter on behalf of all the innocent women, pleading for mercy from the court. Her plea was ignored by the court. The six died at Gallows Hill on September 22.

By September 1692, more than 140 people had been accused of witchcraft and jailed. Nineteen had been sentenced to death by hanging. One was pressed to death; five or six others died in prison. Sarah Osborne was among the few to die in prison before even getting to trial. The cause of her death is unknown.

Giles Corey

Accused of witchcraft, 74-year-old Giles Corey refused to stand trial in the Court of Oyer and Terminer. The villagers brought him outside and laid him on the ground. They piled heavy rocks on top of him to force him to agree to stand trial. They piled more and more rocks on him, but he did not give in. Corey suffocated from the weight of the rocks and died.

Doubts Arise

A group of ten ministers wrote their opinion on the use of spectral evidence. Although they believed these images could identify a witch, they did not feel that spectral evidence could prove that those identified willingly allowed the devil to use his or her body. The ministers believed that the devil was powerful enough to use a person's body against his or her will.

One of the accused women, Mary Easty, had suggested that the accused be interviewed separately. The court took this suggestion and began to question the women in private. After the interviews were closed to the public, things in Salem began to calm down somewhat. During the events of that difficult summer, a segment of the Salem community had grown very concerned about the witch trials. The number of hangings and the still-crowded jail cells suggested that the crisis was not ending. They began

Deaths

Nineteen people accused of witchcraft were hanged on Gallows Hill in 1692:

- June 10: Bridget Bishop
- July 19: Rebecca Nurse, Sarah Good, Susannah Martin, Elizabeth Howe, Sarah Wildes
- August 19: George Burroughs, Martha Carrier, John Willard, George Jacobs Sr., John Proctor
- September 22: Martha Corey, Mary Easty, Ann Pudeator, Alice Parker, Mary Parker, Wilmott Redd, Margaret Scott, and Samuel Wardwell

Others accused of witchcraft died in prison, including Sarah Osborne, Roger Toothaker, Lyndia Dustin, Ann Foster, and possibly one or two others. Various records report different numbers of deaths in prison.

to fear what would happen if the trials were allowed to continue. They bravely came together to fight the court and stop the executions.

On October 3, Increase Mather, a respected Puritan minister, presented a letter to his fellow clergy and the magistrates that discouraged the use of spectral evidence in witchcraft trials. Mather had been following the witch trials and was disturbed by the court's reliance on spectral evidence. He wrote, "It were better that ten suspected witches should escape, than that one innocent person should be condemned."[2]

Several Salem representatives took the letter to Governor Phips. They asked him to step in and stop the witch trials. Governor Phips read Increase Mather's opinion on the spectral evidence. On October 29, Governor Phips dissolved the Court of Oyer and Terminer. The Salem witch crisis was over.

Judge Sewell recants after the Salem witch trials.

Chapter 7

Reverend Cotton Mather

Apologies, Amends, and Reparations

In the weeks and months after the Court of Oyer and Terminer was closed, the magistrates reviewed the cases of all the accused still in jail. Without spectral evidence, few of these cases would hold up. The cases were dismissed.

Condemned women, such as Elizabeth Proctor, were issued pardons and released.

Cotton Mather

Cotton Mather, son of Increase Mather, was one of the most respected ministers in the Massachusetts Bay Colony. He had also been a leader in ensuring that the witch trials took place. Mather attended the trials and hangings in Salem and was a friend of some of the judges. It was Mather who urged the hanging of George Burroughs, even after he had recited the Lord's Prayer perfectly.

Like his father, Cotton Mather was unsure about the use of spectral evidence at trial. However, he disagreed with his father about the outcome of the trials. In October 1692, around the time the Court of Oyer and Terminer was dissolved, Cotton Mather published an account of the witch trials. His book, *Wonders of the Invisible World,* defended the actions of the court.

A Letter

Thomas Brattle was an outspoken opponent of the Salem witch trials. His letter written in 1692 helped convince leaders to end the trials: "What will be the issue of these troubles, God only knows. I am afraid that ages will not wear off that reproach and those stains which these things will leave behind them upon our land. I pray God pity us, humble us, forgive us, and appear mercifully for us in this our mount of distress."[1]

The book was published at a time when many people in Salem began to realize that the witch crisis had been overblown. Cotton Mather acquired a bad reputation for his opinions about the trials, even though many other people had agreed with him earlier.

"I desire to be humbled before God for that sad and humbling providence that befell my father's family in the year of 1692: that I, then being in my childhood, should by such a providence of God, be made an instrument for the accusing of several persons of a grievous crime, whereby their lives were taken away from them, whom now I have just grounds and good reason to believe they were innocent persons; and that it was a great delusion of Satan that deceived me in that sad time, whereby I justly fear that I have been instrumental, with others, though ignorantly and unwitting, to bring upon myself and this land the guilt of innocent blood ..."[2]

—Ann Putnam's apology

Unexplainable Accusations

In the years after the Salem witch trials, the young girls who had been the accusers had a difficult time explaining what had happened. No illness was ever diagnosed that explained the hysteria they suffered. In the aftermath of the crisis, the community still believed witchcraft had affected the girls. At the time, people only questioned the process by which the court had tried the witches.

Though some historians believe the girls invented the fits to get attention, none of the girls ever admitted that they made up the affliction. Still, the whole Salem community held a piece of the blame for the crisis.

Apologies

On January 14, 1697, Massachusetts Bay Colony held a day of fasting and prayer in honor of the people who died. Soon after, magistrate Samuel Sewall, who participated as a judge in the Salem witch trials, apologized for his role in the crisis. He walked into his church and confessed his sin, asking to take the blame for the Salem events and

A Doubter's Account

As the Court of Oyer and Terminer was being dissolved in October 1692, Thomas Brattle, Fellow of the Royal Society of Science, wrote a letter to clergy friends urging them to ensure that the new court be different. News of the Salem crisis had circulated. He wrote of what he had seen:

> *As to the method which the Salem justices do take in their examinations, it is truly this. ... The Justices ask the apprehended why they afflict those poor children, to which the apprehended answer they do not afflict them. The Justices order the apprehended to look upon the said children, which accordingly they do, and at the time of that look (I dare not say by that look as the Salem Gentlemen do), the afflicted are cast into a fit. The apprehended are then blinded and ordered to touch the afflicted and at that touch, though not by the touch (as above), the afflicted ordinarily do come out of their fits. The afflicted persons then declare and affirm that the apprehended have afflicted them, upon which the apprehended persons ... are forthwith committed to prison on suspicion for witchcraft.*[3]

to be forgiven. During the rest of his life, Sewall fought for several important causes. He spoke out against slavery and encouraged peace with the Native Americans.

In the days after Sewall's public apology, 12 men who had served as jurors for the witchcraft trials issued a written apology of their own. Their statement admitted that they had made mistakes in condemning so many people to death. Together, they expressed sorrow for their participation and accepted their share of responsibility for the incidents. They confessed that the evidence they relied on had been insufficient. They referred to biblical passages that suggest that punishing the innocent was an unforgivable sin. Nonetheless, their apology pleaded for forgiveness from God, from the accused, and from their fellow villagers.

"We confess that we ourselves were not capable to understand, nor able to withstand the mysterious delusions of the powers of darkness and prince of the air, but were for want of knowledge in ourselves and better information from other, prevailed with to take up with such evidence against the accused as on further consideration and better information, we justly fear was insufficient for the touching the lives of any. ... We do, therefore, hereby signify to all in general (and to the surviving sufferers in especial) our deep sense of and sorrow for our errors in acting on such evidence to the condemning of any person."[4]

—*Statement from Salem jurors*

The house of Rebecca Nurse

A Change in Ministry

Reverend Samuel Parris also suffered in the wake of the witchcraft crisis. No one could forget that he had become a central figure in the witch hunt when his girls fell ill. Those who were critical of Parris wanted him to apologize for his role in the crisis. He refused. His supporters agreed that he should not have to apologize. The divisions within Salem Village increased.

A team of 17 outsiders came to listen to the grievances of the divisions within Salem and to help solve the problem. Increase Mather, Cotton Mather, and Samuel Willard were among the men who came to mediate the dispute. They arrived in town on April 3, 1695.

Even with outside help, the many years of bitterness could not be resolved. Reverend Parris would have to leave Salem Village. The guest committee helped the town decide on a final payment for Parris before he left town. Parris left by the end of 1697.

The new minister to Salem Village arrived in November 1698. He was a young man named Joseph Green. His arrival helped heal the

Gallows Hill

The site on which the accused witches were executed is known as Gallows Hill. A gallows is a wooden stand designed to hang people. At the time of the witch trials, the hill was believed to be a meeting ground for witches. In the years after the Salem witch trials, residents were known to go to the hill seeking advice from the spirits of the dead witches believed to be lurking in the area. A person would go to the hill at night, speak a question aloud, and listen for the answer to come upon the night wind. The area is still believed to be haunted by the ghosts of those executed.

divisions in the community and gave Salem Village a fresh start. Reverend Green intended to help people learn to forgive each other for the past. He visited the families of those executed and invited them to come to worship. Even though the families would be communing with the accusers, Green convinced them to join in worship. Reverend Green made many small but important changes. He asked all members of the congregation to change seats in church. He placed "enemy" families next to each other in the hope that they would begin to talk and get along. It slowly worked.

Reparations

In 1711, a committee studying the witch trials recommended that the formerly accused witches should receive compensation for their unfair suffering during the trials. The committee also suggested that reparations be paid to the families of the people who were executed.

It took 40 years for some of the families to be compensated. Though the reparations did not make up for the wrongful death of their family members, it was a gesture by the colony to show remorse for the executions.

Exclusion of Hearsay Testimony

The aftermath of the Salem witch trials also led to one of the important principles of law that is still in use today—the exclusion of hearsay as evidence in a lawful trial. Hearsay is a rumor or a retelling of a conversation that a person did not actually witness. Witnesses can only testify to facts, knowledge, and events that they participated in or viewed.

The kind of spectral evidence that was used to condemn witches in Salem would not be allowed in a courtroom today. It would be similar to a witness saying she dreamed about an event and expect the court to believe that the event really occurred. Exclusion of hearsay testimony is an important piece of law that was put in place to help prevent events such as the Salem witch trials from happening again.

A Modeſt Enquiry
Into the Nature of
Witchcraft,

AND

How Perſons Guilty of that Crime may be *Convicted* : And the means uſed for their Diſcovery Diſcuſſed, both *Negatively* and *Affirmatively*, according to *SCRIPTURE* and *EXPERIENCE*.

By John Hale,

Paſtor of the Church of Chriſt in *Beverley*,
Anno Domini 1697.

When they ſay unto you, ſeek unto them that have Familiar Spirits and unto Wizzards, that peep, &c. *To the Law and to the Teſtimony ; if they ſpeak not according to this word, it is becauſe there is no light in them,* Iſaiah VIII. 19, 20.
That which I ſee not teach thou me, Job 34 32.

A Modest Inquiry into the Nature of Witchcraft *was published after the Salem witch trials.*

Chapter 8

Puritans leaving church

What Really Happened at Salem?

Historians and scholars continue to speculate on the Salem witch crisis of 1692. These speculations have resulted in a variety of theories about the girls' illnesses and the reasons for the community's rash and vicious reaction.

It is generally acknowledged that witchcraft was not to blame for the illness. Scholars provide various explanations for the initial fits that overtook the girls.

A Game Gone Awry

One idea is that the afflictions of Betty Parris and her cousin Abigail Williams started as a game among bored children that quickly got out of control. The girls might have gotten the idea after playing with occult spells, or they may simply have been trying to get some attention.

It is possible that Abigail and Betty wanted to play a trick, but it resulted in so much concern from the villagers that they grew to enjoy the attention. The neighboring girls would have been aware of the attention that Abigail and Betty received and may have wanted attention for themselves. It is unlikely that they expected their game to get so out of control.

"When a whole people abandons the solid ground of common sense, overleaps the boundaries of human knowledge, gives itself up to wild reveries, and lets loose its passions without restraint, it presents a spectacle more terrific to behold, and becomes more destructive and disastrous, than any convulsion of mere material nature; than tornado, conflagration or earthquake."[1]

—*Charles W. Upham*

When the community began pressuring the girls to name their tormentors, the girls may not have wanted to admit that it had all been a hoax.

Some historians strongly believe that the girls' hysteria was invented. However, others believe that the eyewitness accounts of the girls' fits provide evidence of real distress.

A Strange Illness

Although they did not participate in the trials the way the girls did, several adult men and women experienced similar symptoms as the girls. Livestock also was observed to be acting peculiar. At the time, the animals' illness was suspected to be the work of witches. Looking back, it indicates that there may have been a widespread outbreak of illness in Salem. Because the affliction affected many people and animals, some historians have explored the idea that the afflictions were caused by some physical illness.

Several scholars have speculated about the possible illnesses. One theory is that there was an outbreak of a serious disease called encephalitis lethargica, which causes hysteria. Symptoms can include headache, double vision, delayed physical response, pains, tremors, and neck rigidity. There is no known cure for encephalitis lethargica, even today. Between 1916 and 1930, the disease swept the world in an epidemic that killed more than 50 million people.

In 1976, psychologist Linnda Caporael suggested a new theory about the girls' hysteria—food poisoning. Caporael believes that the girls might have been infected with a type of food poisoning called convulsive ergotism. Convulsive ergotism occurs when a person eats rye bread that contains a certain moldy growth. It causes hallucinations and other symptoms similar to those the Salem girls

Someone to Blame

Life was hard for many in Salem Village. The villagers faced disease, crop failure, severe weather, and other difficulties that were often beyond their control. They needed somewhere to point the blame, and the blame wound up being placed on those accused of witchcraft.

The process of blaming someone for something that they have no control over is called scapegoating. The term originated in ancient Hebrew society when a priest would place his hands over the head of a goat while reciting the sins of the people. Their sins would be symbolically transferred to the goat and the goat would then be allowed to escape into the wild. As the goat escaped into the wilderness, the community would be cleansed of its sin.

In modern times, scapegoating involves transferring blame to an innocent person or group, as in the case of the Salem witch trials. Although those accused most likely had nothing to do with the girls' fits or any of the other unexplainable occurrences at that time, villagers were desperate to find someone, or something, to blame for their troubles.

experienced. Salem Village residents made and ate rye bread, so it is possible that there is a connection between this mold and the girls' illness. A few other scholars have supported the theory that convulsive ergotism started the Salem crisis. Still, others believe that physical illness is not to blame.

Mental Breakdown

Another theory about the girls' condition suggests that they suffered from a psychological problem. The social circumstances in Salem were very strict. The pressure placed on children to be quiet, well behaved, and respectful to the exclusion of all other emotions and behaviors may have contributed to psychological problems. Girls were expected to suppress feelings of joy, anger, sadness, and curiosity. Historian John Demos and others believe that this repression took its toll on Salem girls. Their fits enabled them to show aggression without being blamed or criticized for their actions. By naming witches, the girls proclaimed themselves innocent of their own actions.

"I am resolved after this never to use but one grain of patience with any man that shall go to impose upon me a denial of devils or of witches."[2]

—*Cotton Mather,* Memorable Providences

Although this theory is similar to the idea that the girls invented the affliction, it is not the same. John Demos does not believe that the girls behaved the way they did on purpose. He believes that the pressures of the social circumstances in Salem unconsciously pushed their brains to react this way.

It is impossible to know which, if any, of these theories is true. Perhaps it was a combination of forces that caused the girls' illnesses.

A Village on Edge

Whether the girls made it up, were infected with rye sickness, or suffered mental distress, these explanations only account for the girls' behavior. They do not explain the community's reaction. They do not explain how the fits of several young girls led to the executions of 20 people. Why did the adults of Salem Village react as they did?

Abracadabra

Abracadabra is a one-word magic spell that people used in medieval times to get rid of sickness or trouble. The word would be written repeatedly, dropping one letter each time (abracadabra, abracadabr, abracadab, abracada, etc.) until the word was gone. The evil force was believed to fade as the word disappeared. Abracadabra was also often used to ward off plague. People would write the word on a scrap of cloth or paper, wear it around the neck for nine days, then throw it over their shoulder into an east-flowing river.

Increase Mather, who was present during the Salem witch trials, believed it to be a powerless "hobgoblin word."[3]

> "All the wild witches, those most noble ladies, / For all their broomsticks and their tears, / Their angry tears, are gone."[4]
>
> —*William Butler Yeats*

Historians believe that Salem Village was ripe for a witch hunt, even before the girls took ill. The prevalence of illness, death, and difficulties within New England society made life challenging and often sorrowful. People did not understand science, weather, illness, and medicine. Belief in witches helped the villagers accept the natural tragedies of early American life. It gave them someone to blame when things did not go well. It gave them a place to point their anger, while allowing them to stay faithful to God and their religion. They did not have to doubt God's mercy, because they had a devil and his servants to blame for their troubles.

There were more accusers than just the afflicted girls. The accusers included people who had suffered illnesses, poor crop seasons, deaths of farm animals, and other circumstances that could have been caused by nature. Although only a few girls started the witch hunt, the village finished it. Accusers from across the village helped keep the witch hunt going.

Historians have tried to determine what caused the witch hunt in Salem.

Chapter 9

A BRIEF and TRUE

NARRATIVE

Of some Remarkable Passages Relating to sundry Persons Afflicted by

VVitchcraft,

AT

SALEM VILLAGE:

Which happened from the Nineteenth of *March*, to the Fifth of *April*, 1692.

Collected by *Deodat Lawson*.

Shortly after the witch trials ended, many people were interested in finding out what had happened in Salem.

What Does Salem Mean to Us Today?

More than 300 years after the Salem witch hunt, historians and scholars continue to study the trials. The witch trials make a fascinating story, but there are other reasons to study the incident. Modern society can still learn from the events of Salem in 1692. The people who lived in Salem led very different lives than Americans do today, but, in most ways, the people themselves were not that different. They worried about their families. They worked hard to make their living. They feared the unknown.

Witch hunts take on many forms, and even 300 years after Salem, they still occur in different ways. Understanding the witch trials of the past may help people understand how to prevent a reoccurrence in the future.

After the Salem Crisis

The people who were tried and hanged at Salem were the last people accused of witchcraft to be killed in the United States. Over time, people stopped believing so strongly in witches. They stopped worrying about curses and spells. Advances in science explained things that had once been thought to be magical. Doctors learned about the causes of disease and developed new treatments. Scientists studied the weather and were able to better predict rain and storms.

However, new fears replaced the old ones. People often continue to be afraid of things that are new or different, especially different kinds of people.

The Puritans came to America to find freedom. They wanted to be in a place where they could live quiet lives and practice their faith. Others began arriving at their shores. In the 1700s and 1800s, thousands of immigrants from Europe arrived, seeking freedom and opportunity. Over time, English, Irish, Italian, French, Germans, and others came to the United States seeking new lives and opportunities. Slave traders began bringing Africans across the ocean to work as slaves on plantations in the South.

It was overwhelming for the young American nation to be made up of so many different people. It was not always easy for people of different backgrounds and cultures to understand each other and get along.

"Witch-hunting is not solely an activity, but also a state of mind that develops when a society is under great stress—and such a state of mind exists today."[1]

—Robert Rapley, witch hunt scholar, 2007

What Makes a Witch Hunt?

The idea of a witch hunt also applies to situations where the person being attacked is not presumed to be an actual witch. The term has gained new meanings over time. A witch hunt describes any situation where a community decides that certain types of people are dangerous and goes to great lengths to find and stop those people.

Witch-hunt scholar Robert Rapley writes, "The most pronounced characteristic of a witch-hunt is that the accused is automatically treated as guilty."[2] The American justice system is based on a system of innocent until proven guilty, but in a witch hunt, those rules change. People assume guilt based on little proof and seek out those they fear for punishment.

The McCarthy Era

One modern example of a witch hunt occurred in the United States in the 1950s. The United States and the Union of Soviet Socialist Republics were pitted against each other in the Cold War. The United States practiced capitalism, a system that values individual work, achievement, and success. The Union of Soviet Socialist Republics practiced communism, a system that valued collective effort and equal sharing of resources. Both countries tried to make their system the preferred form of government across the globe.

During that time, Americans worried about Soviet communists coming to the United States and living among them. A lot of people were very afraid that the Union of Soviet Socialist Republics had sent spies to study American life in order to determine ways to harm the United States. While probably only a few

The Cold War and McCarthy

The Cold War was a military standoff between the communist Soviet Union and the capitalist United States. It lasted from the end of World War II to the collapse of the Soviet Union in the 1990s. Although the conflict never escalated to direct military combat, the two nations battled over support of smaller countries and threatened each other with nuclear retaliation should there be a direct attack.

The Cold War standoff resulted in a fear of communism among American citizens. On February 11, 1950, Senator Joseph McCarthy of Wisconsin sent a telegram to President Eisenhower. He claimed he had a list of more than 200 communists working in the U.S. State Department. This resulted in many people being accused of supporting communism and defending themselves on treason charges. Many people were innocent. Others, who were communist sympathizers, felt that their First Amendment rights were violated.

As chairman of the Senate Permanent Investigation Subcommittee, McCarthy held hearings about hidden communists in the United States. He accused many people of infiltrating the U.S. government, citizenry, and the armed forces. When these hearings began being televised, many Americans felt that McCarthy had gone too far. McCarthy was censured by the Senate on December 2, 1954.

Soviet spies were in the United States, Americans panicked at the thought.

U.S. Senator Joseph McCarthy wanted to rid the country of communists. He launched a search that quickly became a witch hunt. McCarthy and his associates targeted anyone who they believed had any ties to the Communist Party. Friends of known communists were suspected and interviewed. Many artists and successful professionals fell under suspicion because of their political beliefs. Under McCarthy's leadership, the Senate held hearings and trials to convict suspected communists. Suspects were deemed suspicious and forced to name other communists.

Most of the suspected communists were jailed, but a few were put to death on treason charges. Many who were released lost their jobs and suffered from loss of good standing and community support.

The Crucible

In 1952, playwright Arthur Miller wrote *The Crucible*, a play about the Salem witch trials. The witch trials reminded him of what was happening in his own time—the rise of McCarthyism.

America's War on Terror

Some people see the events following the September 11, 2001, terrorist attacks as a more recent example of a witch hunt. After the attacks, Americans became very afraid of terrorists. Among the reactions to the attacks on September 11 was the hunt for more possible terrorists.

Because the September 11 terrorists were Muslim men, many Muslim men fell under suspicion, sometimes without evidence. In October 2001, the U.S.A. PATRIOT Act was signed into law. The act expanded the authority of law enforcement agents in order to prevent terrorism. Hoping to prevent another attack, government officials interviewed and arrested many Muslim men on suspicion of terrorism. Many people of Middle Eastern descent or who appeared to be of Middle Eastern descent were questioned as well. Mosques were raided and people were held for questioning because of their nationality and religious beliefs. Many of the men who were arrested were secretly held for weeks or months. In some cases, even their families and their attorneys were not told where they were being held or allowed to see them. Many Middle Eastern men who were not arrested were the focus of harassment.

Some feel that the government's response was reasonable in this time of chaos and fear. In order to prevent another devastating attack, it was necessary to act quickly. However, the wrongful accusations against so many people during this time of fear reminded some of a witch hunt.

The U.S.A. PATRIOT Act

The U.S.A. PATRIOT Act gives law enforcement and government officers the right to conduct surveillance on citizens as well as access health and educational records. It has allowed non-U.S. citizens to be jailed for months at a time without being charged with any crime or be tried in a court that allows hearsay testimony and secret evidence. It has allowed U.S. citizens to be held in military prisons for months or years without trial.

Many Americans are trying to fight the U.S.A. PATRIOT Act, claiming that it threatens civil liberties and rights guaranteed to Americans by the U.S. Constitution.

The Lesson of Salem

The Salem witch trials offer an important lesson for future generations. The story is special, but not unique. When fear of certain actions drives a community to place blame on individuals, there is a risk of the process turning into a witch hunt. Fear inspires people to rush to judgment. People want the problem solved as soon as possible and are willing to accept an imperfect result. This attitude, however, often results in innocent people being punished.

Studying the history of events such as the Salem witch trials can help societies understand why and how witch hunts happen. With this knowledge, such crises can be prevented from occurring again in the future.

Salem witch trials, 1692

Timeline

1626	1689	1692
Salem is settled in the colony of Massachusetts.	Salem Village Church is established and Samuel Parris arrives in November.	Betty Parris and Abigail Williams begin to experience "fits" in January and February.

1692	1692	1692
Governor Phips sets up the Court of Oyer and Terminer and appoints judges on May 27.	Samuel Sewall requests jury members for the Court of Oyer and Terminer on May 30.	The Court of Oyer and Terminer convenes on June 2; Bridget Bishop is condemned.

1692	1692	1692
Sarah Good, Sarah Osborne, and Tituba are examined on March 1.	George Burroughs is arrested in Maine and brought back to Salem on May 4.	Sir William Phips, the new Massachusetts Bay Colony governor, arrives from England on May 14.

1692	1692	1692
Bridget Bishop is hanged on June 10.	Rebecca Nurse, Susannah Martin, Sarah Good, Sarah Wildes, and Elizabeth Howe are condemned on June 29.	Rebecca Nurse, Susannah Martin, Sarah Good, Sarah Wildes, and Elizabeth Howe are hanged on July 19.

Timeline

1692	1692	1692
Beginning on August 2, five people are condemned over the next four days.	George Jacobs Sr., Martha Carrier, George Burroughs, and John Proctor are hanged August 19.	Martha Corey, Mary Easty, Alice Parker, Ann Pudeator, Dorcas Hoar, and Mary Bradbury are condemned on September 9.

1692	1692	1693
Governor Phips dissolves the Court of Oyer and Terminer on October 29.	Superior Court is created on November 25 to review the remaining witchcraft cases.	Remaining witchcraft cases are reviewed. All cases are dismissed or pardoned.

1692	1692	1692
Court convenes on September 17; nine people are condemned.	On September 19, Giles Corey is pressed to death with rocks for refusing to stand trial.	Eight people are hanged on September 22.

1697	1697
On January 14, Massachusetts Bay Colony observes a day of fasting and prayer in honor of the hanged victims.	Judge Samuel Sewall apologizes.

Essential Facts

Date of Event

1692

Place of Event

Salem, Massachusetts

Key Players

- Reverend Samuel Parris
- Betty Parris
- Abigail Williams
- Sarah Good
- Sarah Osborne
- Tituba
- Governor Phips

Highlights of Event

- Betty Parris and Abigail Williams became afflicted with a strange illness in early 1692. The girls were examined and it was determined that witchcraft was to blame.
- Sarah Good, Sarah Osborne, and Tituba were arrested on suspicion of witchcraft. The women were questioned. Sarah Good and Sarah Osborne denied the charges. Tituba said that she saw the devil and that there were more witches in Salem.
- Nineteen people were executed as witches. Other accused witches died in prison, including Sarah Osborne, Roger Toothaker, Lyndia Dustin, Ann Foster, and as many as two or three others.
- Governor Phips dissolved the Court of Oyer and Terminer on October 29, 1692.

Quote

"I am resolved after this never to use but one grain of patience with any man that shall go to impose upon me a denial of devils or of witches."—*Cotton Mather,* Memorable Providences

Additional Resources

Select Bibliography

Boyer, Paul and Stephen Nissenbaum. *Salem Possessed*. Cambridge, MA: Harvard University Press, 1974.

Breslaw, Elaine, ed. *Witches of the Atlantic World*. New York: New York University Press, 2000.

Norton, Mary Beth. *In the Devil's Snare*. New York: Alfred A. Knopf, 2002.

Rapley, Robert. *Witch Hunts: From Salem to Guantanamo Bay*. Montreal: McGill-Queens University Press, 2007.

Further Reading

Aronson, Marc. *Witch-Hunt: Mysteries of the Salem Witch Trials*. New York: Simon and Schuster, 2005.

Fraustino, Lisa Rowe. *I Walk in Dread*. New York: Scholastic, 2004.

Orr, Tamra B. *The Salem Witch Trials*. New York: Thomson Gale, 2003.

Rinaldi, Ann. *A Break with Charity: A Story about the Salem Witch Trials*. New York: Harcourt, 2003.

Web Links

To learn more about the Salem witch trials, visit ABDO Publishing Company on the World Wide Web at **www.abdopublishing.com**. Web sites about the Salem witch trials are featured on our Book Links page. These links are routinely monitored and updated to provide the most current information available.

Places To Visit

Salem Witch Museum
Washington Square, Salem, Massachusetts 01970
978-744-1692
www.salemwitchmuseum.com
Exhibits cover the history of the Salem witch trials, the practice of modern witchcraft, and examples of witch hunts.

Witch Dungeon Museum
16 Lynde Street, Salem, Massachusetts 01970
978-741-3570
www.witchdungeon.com/witchdungeon.html
Exhibits include a live reenactment of a Salem witch trial and a tour of a dungeon similar to one where the accused were imprisoned.

Witch History Museum
197-201 Essex Street, Salem, Massachusetts 01970
978-741-7770
www.witchhistorymuseum.com
Includes 15 exhibits reenacting life in Old Salem Village.

Glossary

accused

A person who is blamed for causing something to happen or thought to be guilty of a crime.

affliction

An illness.

devil

The believed source of evil and witchcraft powers.

familiar

An animal helper that works with and on behalf of a witch to bring evil.

fit

A sudden attack of illness involving seizures, convulsions, and hallucinations.

gallows

A special stand, usually built from wood, where condemned prisoners were brought to be hanged.

Goody

Short for Goodwife, a title of respect given to women in Puritan communities, similar to the way "Mrs." is used today.

hearsay

Rumors; something a witness was told by someone else but did not personally witness.

hysteria

A crazed attitude of fear; an illness leading to mental distress.

magistrate

A judge or a lawyer with power to enforce laws in the community.

paralysis

Inability to move.

persecute

To harass or punish people, often because of their race or religious beliefs.

placebo

A substance that has no medical benefit but may be prescribed for psychological benefits.

reformation

Religious movement to reform or modify certain religious practices or doctrines.

reparation

A payment made to make amends to someone who has been wronged.

seizure

A sudden physical attack such as convulsions, loss of senses, and/or loss of consciousness resulting from disease.

spectral evidence

Visions and other magical testimony that was considered evidence of witchcraft.

testify

To state knowledge of evidence before a judge and jury.

voodoo

A Haitian religion.

witch

A person who possesses magical powers and puts them to use either for good or for evil.

witch hunt

A searching out and persecution of individuals who are perceived as threats.

Source Notes

Chapter 1. Turning Point

1. Elaine Breslaw, ed. *Witches of the Atlantic World*. New York: New York University Press, 2000. 390.

2. Paul Boyer and Stephen Nissenbaum, eds. *The Salem Witchcraft Papers*. Charlottesville, VA: The Rectors and Visitors of the University of Virginia, 2002. Vol. 2. 357. 15 Aug. 2007 <http://etext.virginia.edu/salem/witchcraft/texts/BoySal2.html>.

3. The Holy Bible. King James Version. New York: American Bible Society. 1999, Exodus 22:18, Bartleby.com, 2000. 2 Oct. 2007 <www.bartleby.com>.

Chapter 2. Social Context

1. Mary Beth Norton. *In the Devil's Snare*. New York: Alfred A. Knopf, 2002. 15.

2. The Holy Bible. King James Version. New York: American Bible Society. 1999, 1 Peter 5:8, Bartleby.com, 2000. 2 Oct. 2007 <www.bartleby.com>.

3. Ibid. Exodus 22:18.

Chapter 3. Historical Persecution of Witches

None.

Chapter 4. Afflictions Emerge

1. Mary Beth Norton. *In the Devil's Snare*. New York: Alfred A. Knopf, 2002. 26.

2. Ibid. 26.

3. Elaine Breslaw, ed. *Witches of the Atlantic World*. New York: New York University Press, 2000. 390.

Chapter 5. Naming Witches

1. Laurie Winn Carlson. *A Fever in Salem*. Chicago: Ivan R. Dee, 1999. xiii.

Chapter 6. Hangings

1. "Salem Witch Trials—the People—Sarah Good." *Discovery School*. 15 Aug. 2007 <http://school.discovery.com/schooladventures/salemwitchtrials/people/good.html>.

2. Robert Rapley. *Witch Hunts: From Salem to Guantanamo Bay*. Montreal: McGill-Queens University Press, 2007. 96.

Chapter 7. Apologies, Amends, and Reparations

1. Elaine Breslaw, ed. *Witches of the Atlantic World*. New York: New York University Press, 2000. 419.

2. Frances Hill. *The Salem Witch Trials Reader*. Cambridge, MA: DaCapo Press, 2000. 108.

3. Elaine Breslaw, ed. *Witches of the Atlantic World*. New York: New York University Press, 2000. 412.

4. Ibid.

Chapter 8. What Really Happened at Salem?

1. Charles W. Upham. *Salem Witchcraft*. Mineola, NY: Dover, 2000. 313.

2. "Salem Witch Trials—the People—Cotton Mather." *Discovery School*. 15 Aug. 2007 <http://school.discovery.com/schooladventures/salemwitchtrials/people/mather.html>.

3. Rosemary Ellen Guiley. *The Encyclopedia of Witches and Witchcraft*. 2nd ed. New York: Checkmark Books, 1999. 1.

4. Robert Rapley. *Witch Hunts: From Salem to Guantanamo Bay*. Montreal: McGill-Queens University Press, 2007. 3.

Chapter 9. What Does Salem Mean to Us Today?

1. Robert Rapley. *Witch Hunts: From Salem to Guantanamo Bay*. Montreal: McGill-Queens University Press, 2007. ix.

2. Ibid.

Index

About the Author

Kekla Magoon has a Master of Fine Arts in Writing for Children and Young Adults from Vermont College. Her work includes many different kinds of writing, but she especially enjoys writing historical fiction and nonfiction. When she is not writing books for children, she works with nonprofit organizations and helps with fundraising for youth programs.

Photo Credits

North Wind Picture Archives, cover, 3, 6, 13, 14, 18, 25, 26, 36, 38, 45, 46, 55, 56, 63, 67, 68, 73, 77, 78, 85, 86, 95, 96, 97, 98, 99; MPI/Getty Images, 21; Imagno/Getty Images, 30; Hulton Archive/Getty Images, 35.